This devotional reveals the deep
Israel. It draws the reader into di.
His people. Day after day, it unveils His motives and heart's longing.
It shows the richness of God's love as a Father, Shepherd,
Bridegroom, and King toward His Beloved Israel.

Pierre has been faithfully praying for Israel for over 20 years. He is
the real deal.

The Scripture explicitly exhorts us to pray for peace for Jerusalem
in Psalms 122. Furthermore, the Apostle Paul clearly emphasizes the
importance of the salvation of Jewish people in Romans 9-11 as part
of God's redemptive purpose. This 21-day devotional provides daily
manna and scripturally rooted prayer guidance for us to agree with
the Holy Spirit and one another on a 21-day focus to join His heart
for Israel at this crucial hour of redemptive history. I highly
recommend it.

As followers of Jesus, devoted to God's Word, we are repeatedly
encouraged in Scripture to take part in seeing the Lord's purposes
for Israel come to fullness. Isaiah 62 reminds us of our role as
"watchmen on (Jerusalem's) walls..." until her salvation is "as a
burning torch." David charges us to "Pray for the peace of

Jerusalem" (Psalm 122:6). These exhortations, and dozens more like them, are certainly related to the general well-being of Israel. But even more, they encompass the *ultimate salvation* of Israel (Romans 11:25) as well as seeing Jewish people come to faith in Yeshua *now* in our day.

We can face a challenge, at times, with knowing the *specifics* of what to pray. Pierre Bezençon has provided a great blessing to the body of Messiah in putting together this powerful 21-day prayer devotional, "The Heart of God for Israel." Far more than simply a prayer *list*, this book takes us on a journey into the very *heart* of God, giving us a wonderful tool for partnering with the Lord through our intercession. Each day of the devotional serves as a foundation for launching us into our own *spontaneous* praying. I strongly recommend this devotional for assisting God's people in our *passion* and our *praying* for God's work in Israel in these last days.

Rabbi Jerry Miller, Grace Empowers Ministries

Pierre Bezençon's work is excellent on many levels: it is biblically balanced and radical all at the same time; it connects us to the mainline heart of the Father for the Jewish people; it is a joy to read. I am delighted to recommend it as a guide for prayer!

Avner Boskey, Final Frontier Ministries, Beersheva/Nashville

THE HEART OF GOD FOR ISRAEL

A 21-Day Devotional

Pierre Bezençon

Homes of Love

WEEK 1

GOD'S LOVE LANGUAGE TOWARD ISRAEL

WEEK 2

GOD'S COVENANTS WITH ISRAEL

WEEK 3

GOD'S LOVE FOR JERUSALEM

WEEK 1

GOD'S LOVE LANGUAGE FOR ISRAEL

He expresses His affection in some of the strongest emotions of the human experience.

DAY 1

YOUR MAKER IS YOUR HUSBAND

"For your Maker is your husband, the LORD of hosts is his name; and the Holy One of Israel is your Redeemer, the God of the whole earth he is called. For the LORD has called you like a wife forsaken and grieved in spirit, like a wife of youth when she is cast off, says your God. For a brief moment I forsook you, but with great compassion I will gather you. In overflowing wrath for a moment I hid my face from you, but with everlasting love I will have compassion on you, says the LORD, your Redeemer."

Isaiah 54:5-8 RSV

God expresses His love for Israel in marital declarations. A happy and lifelong marriage seems like a universal aspiration of the human heart. The desire to find a good and faithful spouse springs from the depths of our humanity. Stories of love fascinate young and old, male and female alike.

God chooses to use such passionate love language to convey the intensity of His love for Israel. Your Maker is your husband! This declaration is so strong, so personal, so intimate! The Creator of all things declares that He is in a covenantal relationship with the sons of Israel. He is Israel's faithful Husband. God is her Strength, Defender, and Provider forever.

God doesn't want Israel to misunderstand Him. He has not forsaken her. His love is everlasting; His anger only lasts for a moment. His temporary discipline is part of His eternal commitment and zeal toward Israel. With great compassion, I will gather you. I will have compassion for you with everlasting love, says the Lord, your Redeemer.

Prayer

Our Father,

We bless Your Holy Name. We praise You for Your everlasting love for Israel. You are a Husband to her. We thank You because, in Messiah, we have been grafted into the Olive tree. Thus, we share the inheritance of Israel. We thank You for Your Son, the Bridegroom, who gave His life for His Bride (Eph 5:25).

We pray that You will encounter the Jewish people through Your Holy Spirit. Let them see that even when they felt that You had abandoned them in the Holocaust, You have kept Your everlasting love and compassion for them.

In the name of Jesus. Amen.

DAY 2

THE PERPETUAL FRESH LOVE OF A FIANCÉ TOWARD HIS FIANCÉE

"And I will betroth you to me forever; I will betroth you to me in righteousness and in justice, in steadfast love, and in mercy. I will betroth you to me in faithfulness; and you shall know the LORD."

Hosea 2:19-20 RSV

13

There is a matchless excitement associated with getting engaged. Feelings of love fly high as the engagement draws near. Mutual admiration, passionate desire, and untainted joy fill the heart of the future bride and bridegroom. They experience a unique blend of freshness, innocence, and hope for the future. They are so focused on each other that the surroundings seem to vanish. The doors of blissful love are wide open in front of them.

God promised to betroth Israel when she was behaving like a prostitute. His jealous love ends up making everything new. His undeserved tenacious affection transforms the future of Israel. God does not condemn His Bride. He wants her for Him alone, free from all her other lovers. She is neither rejected nor disqualified. Israel is loved, and yes, loved <u>forever</u>!

God expresses His emotions with the language of engagement. He is not bored or burdened. He is not keeping His covenant reluctantly because of a sense of duty. He is still passionate about his bride. His conquering love passes over any heartbreaking disappointments. Israel is so precious to Him. He will not let her go. He will not let strangers seduce her. He will bring her into His world of righteousness, steadfast love, and mercy. Israel will be transformed and will know Him. Whatever the past, God opens a bright future for His Beloved Israel.

Prayer

Our Father,

We bless Your Holy Name. We thank You for Your everlasting love for Israel. Thank you for letting us understand Your feelings for Israel. You express Your zealous affection with some of the strongest emotions of the human heart.

We pray for the Jewish people, specifically those who think they have gone too far from You. Let them know who You are. Let them know Your heart for them. Let them know that you are ready to write a new story with them and that they have a bright future with You.

Give compassion and boldness to the Body of Messiah worldwide to share the Good News of Your character with them. Raise many faithful witnesses to reach out to the Jewish people.

In the Name of Jesus. Amen

DAY 3

TENDER AS A MOTHER
TOWARD HER BABY

"But Zion said, "The LORD has forsaken me, my Lord has forgotten me." "Can a woman forget her sucking child, that she should have no compassion on the son of her womb? Even these may forget, yet I will not forget you. Behold, I have graven you on the palms of my hands; your walls are continually before me."

Isaiah 49:14-16 RSV

17

God expresses His never changing love toward Jerusalem with some of the most powerful feelings of the human heart. A mother cannot forget her sucking baby. She cannot be indifferent to her hungry, weeping child. Even if a woman doesn't care for the son of her womb, God will never forget nor forsake Zion. He loves her with the tenderness and attention of a loving mother.

God has graven Jerusalem on His palms. Zion, and by extension, Israel, is inscribed on God's hands. This declaration takes its full meaning in the light of the pierced hands of the Messiah at Golgotha. Jesus died first (but not only) for the lost sheep of the house of Israel. Jerusalem's walls are continually before Him. Israel is at the center of His attention and care.

Fingerprints and palm lines are unique to each person. They can be used to identify someone with accuracy. Zion is in God's heart. He has linked Himself to her. His love for Jerusalem describes who He is and reveals His identity. God engraved Israel on His palms. God and Israel are indissociable.

Prayer

Our Father,

We bless Your Holy Name. We praise You for Your unceasing tenderness and care for Zion. You have bound Yourself to Israel. Jerusalem has all your attention. Her walls are continually before You. You will never forget her. You have bound Yourself to her forever.

Give us a revelation of the place of Israel within Your heart. Show the Body of Christ how important Zion is in Your eyes. Lead us into mature love; we want to love You and love the sons of Israel that You love tenderly. We want to know You as the God who loves Jerusalem tenderly. Your love for her reveals Your character. Help us know Your heart better.

In the Name of Jesus. Amen

DAY 4

ISRAEL IS MY SON

"Then you shall say to Pharaoh, 'Thus says the LORD: "Israel is My son, My firstborn. "So, I say to you, let My son go that he may serve Me. But if you refuse to let him go, indeed I will kill your son, your firstborn."'

Exodus 4:22-23 NKJV

God declares that Israel is His firstborn son. At that time, the sons of Jacob had multiplied to form a nation. God states that He is the Father of the nation of Israel. He does not speak about an individual but a people. Nevertheless, His fatherly relationship with such a large group is neither impersonal nor aloof. God draws a parallel between His firstborn son and Pharaoh's firstborn son.

As a father takes on the neighborhood bully because he cannot let his children suffer another abuse, God takes on Pharaoh. He does not tolerate crimes against His son – the sons of Jacob, any longer. He rises against the shedding of innocent blood. He puts a stop to the murderous politics of the king of Egypt. He says: "No more genocide! No more slaughtering of My firstborn son – the descendants of My friend Abraham! If you keep doing this, I will kill your firstborn son! You will experience what I feel when you mistreat them!"

Pharaoh had to face God's wrath when he touched Israel. What happens to Israel is very personal to God. It's not business; it's family! God stands to defend and protect His firstborn son.

Prayer

Our Father,

We bless Your Holy Name. We praise You for Your fatherly love for the nation of Israel. We thank You for rising and defending Your firstborn son. Thank you for contending with those who bullied Your people. You are a good Father to Israel.

We pray for the Body of Messiah to embrace Israel as God's firstborn son and acknowledge that no one can take his place. We pray that the worldwide Church will admit that she is a branch – not the root –grafted into the Olive tree of Israel.

We pray for the Church to stand with the children of Israel and not against them. We pray for believers worldwide to align with God's will for the Jewish people. We pray that the Body of Christ will stand firm against any form of anti-Semitism.

In the Name of Jesus. Amen

DAY 5

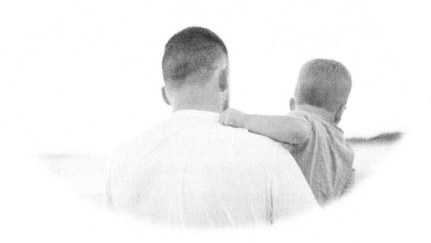

LIKE A FATHER
CARRYING HIS SON

"'The LORD your God, who goes before you, He will fight for you, according to all He did for you in Egypt before your eyes, 'and in the wilderness where you saw how the LORD your God carried you, as a man carries his son, in all the way that you went until you came to this place.' "Yet, for all that, you did not believe the LORD your God, "who went in the way before you to search out a place for you to pitch your tents, to show you the way you should go, in the fire by night and in the cloud by day."

Deuteronomy 1:30-33 NKJV

25

God expresses His love for Israel in the language of a Father taking good care of His son. God is to Israel everything that a good father is to his young son.

God leads the way. He doesn't send His children wandering helplessly in the desert of life. God provides orientation and direction to His family.

He fights for His children. Acting as a Father, He doesn't leave them defenseless. He watches that no one will prey on them. He carries His firstborn son on His shoulders when he has no more strength to walk in the wilderness. He bears the weaknesses of His people.

God goes before Israel to search for a place for them to pitch their tents. He goes ahead and prepares a place of rest and safety. He displays His fatherly care in every possible way toward Israel, thus revealing His emotions.

God is so near Israel. He walks with her and shares her existence and circumstances. As a Father, God is neither distant nor indifferent. He is the opposite of an absent father. God is actively involved in Israel's life journey. He continually brings positive and helpful input.

Prayer

Our Father,

We bless Your Holy Name. We praise You for demonstrating Your fatherly love to Israel in many practical ways. Your care reveals who You are. You delight in being actively involved in the life of the children of Israel. You help the weary. You defend the weak. You go before Your people and show the way. You enjoy walking with them and surrounding them with safety. It breaks Your heart when they reject Your helping hand. It causes You sadness when they want to walk without You.

Reveal Yourself to the Jewish people. Let them know that You desire a Father to son relationship and a Father to daughter relationship with them. Show them that Jesus the Messiah is the only Way to You, that He is the access point to Your Father's heart. Let them see they can enter into an intimate relationship with You by believing in their Messiah.

Make known Your tender care for Israel to the Body of Christ. Show us how much You love Your firstborn son. Impart Your love for Israel to our hearts.

In the Name of Jesus. Amen.

DAY 6

ISRAEL IS GOD'S
INHERITANCE

"For the LORD's portion is his people, Jacob his allotted heritage. "He found him in a desert land, and in the howling waste of the wilderness; he encircled him, he cared for him, he kept him as the apple of his eye. Like an eagle that stirs up its nest, that flutters over its young, spreading out its wings, catching them, bearing them on its pinions, the LORD alone did lead him, and there was no foreign god with him."

Deuteronomy 32:9-12 RSV

29

Israel is God's portion. Jacob is His inheritance. What a statement of worth and appreciation! What a declaration of belonging!

We often say that God is our portion and heritage, and that is true. We see Him as the greatest gift of all, above all the blessings and eternal rewards He bestows on us. Here, Israel is the inheritance of God. Jacob enriches God as children enrich their parents. Israel is His treasure, as kids are their mothers' and fathers' gems. What a powerful proclamation of value! What a fantastic assertion of significance in God's eye.

God expresses His love for Israel in the language of an eagle caring for its young. It is only by His attentive care that Jacob survived in a hostile wilderness. God surrounded Israel with protection. He cared for him and kept him as the apple of His eye. Like the apple of the eye, Israel is very personal, sensitive, and precious to God. Whatever distress Israel experiences affects the Lord intimately.

Like an eagle training its young to fly, watching over them carefully, and backing them every step of the way, God teaches Israel to trust and follow Him. He supplies strength and assistance with patience whenever Jacob is in need. He will not let Israel fall down but catches her and bears her on His wings.

Prayer

Our Father,

We bless Your Holy Name. We praise You for your love for Israel. Thank you for letting us know that Jacob is Your inheritance and the sons of Israel are so precious to You. Thank you for showing us how closely You watch over and tenderly care for them. Thank you for grafting us into the Olive tree of Israel through Jesus the Messiah, making us Your inheritance, too.

Let the Body of Christ know that Israel is the apple of Your eye. Open the understanding of the believers and impart your emotions to them. Share Your heart with Your Church. Lead us to surround the Jewish people with our love and prayers. Let us take good care of them when an opportunity arises and stand with them in times of trouble.

In the Name of Jesus. Amen

DAY 7

THE GOOD SHEPHERD OF ISRAEL

"He will feed his flock like a shepherd, he will gather the lambs in his arms, he will carry them in his bosom, and gently lead those that are with young."

Isaiah 40:11 RSV

God is depicted here as a kind and tender shepherd who deals gently with Israel. His behavior could be instantly understood by most people in Israel, as many were shepherds. This language was very close to their daily experience. They could "see" the heart of a shepherd toward his sheep in the reflection of his actions. They knew from the inside that these gestures were pointing at a patient, generous, and caring soul.

The Shepherd of Israel provides for all, but He is uniquely affectionate toward the little ones. He takes special care of the weak. He does not push the vulnerable; He carries them.

God encourages, protects, and comforts Israel in her times of distress. He does not overlook the defenseless and the feeble. He takes more upon Himself so they can cope with difficult situations. God bears their weaknesses.

The heart of a leader transpires through his dealing with the little ones. God shows the beauty of His character in this scripture. He is humble and gentle, meek and lowly. *"Blessed is the nation whose God is the LORD, the people whom he has chosen as his heritage!"* (Psalm 33:12 RSV)

Prayer

Our Father,

We bless Your Holy Name. We praise You, Good Shepherd. We thank You for Your tender care for the children of Israel. You make known Your character in dealing gently with the little ones of Israel. You welcome the weak into your arms and carry them close to Your heart. Your care reveals who You are.

We pray for the Jewish people. Open their eyes to Your tender affection. Let them see You rightly. Break the lies that distort Your face. Let them see You as the Good Shepherd. Let them see You as the Father who sent Jesus the Messiah to represent You in the flesh. Draw them to Your Son; attract them to Your heart.

In the Name of Jesus. Amen.

WEEK 2

GOD'S COVENANTS WITH ISRAEL

*He is the faithful God, keeping
His covenant of love to a
thousand generations.*

DAY 8

GOD HAS ESTABLISHED AN EVERLASTING COVENANT WITH ISRAEL

"And I will establish my covenant between me and you and your descendants after you throughout their generations for an everlasting covenant, to be God to you and to your descendants after you."

Genesis 17:7 RSV

"God said, "No, but Sarah your wife shall bear you a son, and you shall call his name Isaac. I will establish my covenant with him as an everlasting covenant for his descendants after him."

Genesis 17:19 RSV

39

God made a unique pact with His friend Abraham. He has established an <u>everlasting</u> covenant with him and his descendants, in which He promised to be their God. This covenant is transferred to Isaac, but Ishmael received a blessing as a son of Abraham.

God bound Himself to the sons of Jacob in a unique way. He became their God, and Israel became His people forever. His covenant is the red thread of His story with them. His faithfulness to His covenantal promises is the "why" behind the "what."

God keeps rescuing and loving His people even when they rebel and repeatedly reject Him. His discipline is an integral part of His faithfulness. God will not let them go astray without calling them back to Him. He pursues His people and continually offers them a fresh start even after their stubborn disobedience. Even if God uses the rod of judgment against Israel temporarily, He persists in welcoming them back over and over again.

Prayer

Our Father,

We bless Your Holy Name. We praise You for your everlasting covenant with Israel. We are so grateful to see Your faithfulness generation after generation. You have been loyal to Israel. We can rely on Your fidelity toward us as we are part of the New Covenant. You will never give up on us. We worship You.

Open the eyes of Your Church worldwide to Your everlasting covenant with Israel. Let the Body of Christ see that the sons of Jacob have a unique place in Your heart because of Your covenant with Your friend Abraham. Lead the believers to pray for those You love.

Teach us to "read" Your discipline toward Israel as a manifestation of Your faithfulness. Help us to rightly interpret Your dealings with Your ancient covenantal people. Let us see that You keep pursuing them generation after generation.

In the Name of Jesus. Amen.

DAY 9

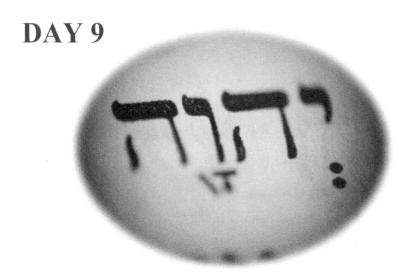

I AM, GOD OF ABRAHAM, ISAAC, AND JACOB. THIS IS MY NAME FOREVER

"Then Moses said to God, "Indeed, when I come to the children of Israel and say to them, 'The God of your fathers has sent me to you,' and they say to me, 'What is His name?' what shall I say to them?" And God said to Moses, "I AM WHO I AM." And He said, "Thus you shall say to the children of Israel, 'I AM has sent me to you.'" Moreover God said to Moses, "Thus you shall say to the children of Israel: 'The LORD God of your fathers, the God of Abraham, the God of Isaac, and the God of Jacob, has sent me to you. This is My name forever, and this is My memorial to all generations.'"

Exodus 3:13-15 NKJV

43

First, God defines Himself as "I AM WHO I AM." He is the existing One, the absolute, never changing, eternal Being. He is the Creator of everything that exists. Then, God identifies Himself as the God of Abraham, the God of Isaac, and the God of Jacob. He is the One that revealed Himself to them and made a covenant with them. God concludes His presentation by stating: "This is My name forever." Because of its direct textual proximity, "this" refers to both "YHWH" and "the God of Abraham, the God of Isaac, and the God of Jacob."

God wants to be known as the One nobody can define perfectly except Himself - "I AM WHO I AM" or "YHWH." However, He chooses to be identified by His relationship with His covenantal friends. The Creator of all things, the God of the Universe, wants to be recognized forever as the God who befriended Abraham, Isaac, and Jacob and made a covenant with them. This passage shows how much God values relationships and honors His covenant with those He created in His image.

God is neither "the unknowable Creator" nor "the undefined Supreme Being." His covenant with Abraham, Isaac, and Jacob paves the way for those who seek a living relationship with their Creator. He has revealed Himself to His friends and wants to be known by those who walk in their steps. Much more so, God wants to be known through His Son, Jesus the Messiah.

Prayer

Our Father,

We bless Your Holy Name. We praise You, the Great I AM. We worship You for making Yourself known to Abraham, Isaac, and Jacob. Thank you for establishing a covenant with them. Thank you for making Your Name famous <u>forever</u>: YHWH, the God of Abraham, the God of Isaac, and the God of Jacob. Thank you for revealing Yourself ultimately in Your Son, Jesus.

We pray that You will wake Israel to the reality that they belong to You and that You are their God forever. We pray they will know their identity and calling is to be Yours. We pray they will return to You and leave their attempts to self-define themselves.

We pray that the Church worldwide will understand that the roots of her faith go back to Your covenant with Israel. Let her see the new covenant as part of God's redemptive story that He began with the patriarchs.

In the Name of Jesus. Amen.

DAY 10

THEY SAW THE GOD OF ISRAEL

"Then Moses went up, also Aaron, Nadab, and Abihu, and seventy of the elders of Israel, and they saw the God of Israel. And there was under His feet as it were a paved work of sapphire stone, and it was like the very heavens in its clarity. But on the nobles of the children of Israel He did not lay His hand. So they saw God, and they ate and drank."

Exodus 24:9-11 NKJV

God revealed Himself shortly after His covenant with the people on Mount Sinai. In this extraordinary epiphany, He is identified as the God of Israel. He wants to make Himself known as the God of Israel. The Creator of the Universe, the All-Mighty, I AM WHO I AM chooses to bear the name of His people. What incredible humility! What a powerful statement of unity! What a stunning declaration of love!

God, for the sake of love, takes the name of His people in the same way a bride receives the name of her bridegroom through the bond of marriage. God and Israel are one through the covenant, like husband and wife become one. They are no longer two but one. God's destiny and Israel's destiny are linked forever.

This story speaks of God's character. He is not afraid to embrace who we are for the sake of love. God is ready to join Himself – through a covenant – to our humanity. He fully demonstrated this through His Son Jesus, who shared our human condition to clothe us with His divine glory.

Prayer

Our Father,

We bless Your Holy Name. We praise You, the Creator of all things, for making Yourself known as the God of Israel. We thank You for showing us the extent of Your love for Israel and, by extension, for us. Your desire to partner with us through a covenant is beyond our understanding, yet our hearts grasp Your fantastic offer of love.

We pray that You will grant us a more profound revelation of Your covenants. Show us the power of Your covenantal promises with Israel and instruct us to honor them. Open the eyes of our hearts to see how faithful You are to Your covenants. Teach us how to walk in them.

Let Your Church worldwide see that she loves the God of Israel (Mark 12:29) and follow the Messiah of Israel.

In the Name of Jesus. Amen

DAY 11

GOD KEEPS HIS COVENANTS WITH JACOB AND DAVID

"The word of the LORD came to Jeremiah: "Have you not observed what these people are saying, 'The LORD has rejected the two families which he chose'? Thus, they have despised my people so that they are no longer a nation in their sight. Thus says the LORD: If I have not established my covenant with day and night and the ordinances of heaven and earth, then I will reject the descendants of Jacob and David my servant and will not choose one of his descendants to rule over the seed of Abraham, Isaac, and Jacob. For I will restore their fortunes and will have mercy upon them.""

Jeremiah 33:23-26 RSV

51

The rejection or the replacement of Israel is not a new topic. The intensity of God's judgment on Israel over the centuries has made many wonder if God was still in covenant with Israel. The exile, the first destruction of Jerusalem, and the absence of a king on the throne of David opened a crisis of faith within the people. Were the dramatic events showing that God had ended His covenant because of the many sins of His people?

God addresses the issue through the prophet Jeremiah. He rebukes the people who say that the Lord has rejected the families of Jacob, Israel, and David – the royal line. God confirms His covenants with the two families that He chose.

The Lord uses powerful language. His covenants with them are as strong as the cosmic order He set in place. He will not reject them as long as day and night exist. God will have mercy upon them as long as the fixed order of heaven and earth stands. He has established immutable cosmic laws visible in the created order; similarly, His covenants with Israel and David are irreversible. Israel will remain God's firstborn son, and the son of David – Jesus – will sit on the Messianic throne in Jerusalem forever.

Prayer

Our Father,

We bless Your Holy Name. We thank You for Your faithfulness to Your covenants with Israel. You are true to Your words. You are faithful to Your promises. You always keep Your part of the covenants You established with Your people.

We pray that the Jewish people will return to Your covenants, see Your faithfulness despite the tragedies they have experienced, and see You as You indeed are.

We pray that You give us a deeper understanding of Your covenants. Grant us to know You as the covenant-keeping God. Anchor our faith in the solid foundations of Your covenants so we will be unshakable when everything shakes.

In the Name of Jesus. Amen.

DAY 12

GOD'S COVENANT WITH DAVID

"'Behold, the days are coming,' says the LORD, 'that I will perform that good thing which I have promised to the house of Israel and to the house of Judah: 'In those days and at that time I will cause to grow up to David A Branch of righteousness; He shall execute judgment and righteousness in the earth. In those days Judah will be saved, And Jerusalem will dwell safely. And this is the name by which she will be called: THE LORD OUR RIGHTEOUSNESS.' "For thus says the LORD: 'David shall never lack a man to sit on the throne of the house of Israel."

Jeremiah 33:14-17 NKJV

God is faithful to perform <u>that</u> good thing He promised to the house of Israel and <u>Judah</u>. That good thing is a Branch of righteousness growing up in the house of David, namely the coming of the Messiah. The Father sent Jesus to fulfill this promise made to <u>Israel</u>. When Jesus executes judgment and establishes righteousness in the earth, God will save Judah, and Jerusalem will dwell safely.

Zachariah, the father of John the Baptist, summarized the appearing of Jesus in these words: "Blessed be the Lord God of Israel, for he has visited and redeemed his people, and has raised up a horn of salvation for us in the house of his servant David, as he spoke by the mouth of his holy prophets from of old, that we should be saved from our enemies, and from the hand of all who hate us; to perform the mercy promised to our fathers, and to remember his holy covenant," (Luke 1:68-72 RSV)

The whole storyline revolves around the people who are in covenant with God. The house of Israel and the house of Judah, King David, and his throne, the salvation of Judah and Jerusalem, are at the center of God's promise. The son of David will sit on his ancestor's throne in Jerusalem. The King of kings will also rule from that city.

The coming of the Messiah takes place in Israel's storyline. All of God's promises to Israel converge and point to Jesus. Israel and Jerusalem are not marginalized, nor have they become realities of the past. God plans to exalt His Son in direct connection to His relationship with Israel. The nations drawn and saved by Jesus are joined to Israel's covenants and promises.

Prayer

Our Father,

We bless Your Holy Name. We praise You for Your covenant with the house of Israel and the house of Judah, and Your faithfulness in fulfilling Your promise. We thank You for Jesus, the Branch of Righteousness born in the house of David. We wait with great expectation to see him execute judgment and righteousness on the earth from Jerusalem. We long to see Jerusalem called THE LORD OUR RIGHTEOUSNESS.

We pray that Your worldwide Church will understand that Israel remains in the picture till the end because of Your faithfulness to Your covenants. Show the Church that Israel will play a central role in end-time events as Jesus is the Messiah of Israel as well as the Savior of the nations.

We pray that You will open the eyes of the Jewish people to recognize that Jesus is the Messiah they have been waiting for. We pray You will call and send more messengers to Israel to share the Good News. We pray for You to strengthen and anoint those already preaching the gospel of peace to the Jewish people (Romans 10:14-15).

In the Name of Jesus. Amen.

DAY 13

GOD'S NEW COVENANT WITH THE HOUSE OF ISRAEL

""Behold, the days are coming, says the LORD, when I will make a new covenant with the house of Israel and the house of Judah, not like the covenant which I made with their fathers when I took them by the hand to bring them out of the land of Egypt, my covenant which they broke, though I was their husband, says the LORD. But this is the covenant which I will make with the house of Israel after those days, says the LORD: I will put my law within them, and I will write it upon their hearts; and I will be their God, and they shall be

my people. And no longer shall each man teach his neighbor and each his brother, saying, 'Know the LORD,' for they shall all know me, from the least of them to the greatest, says the LORD; for I will forgive their iniquity, and I will remember their sin no more."'

Jeremiah 31:31-34 RSV

God makes the New Covenant with the house of <u>Israel</u> and Judah. The nations are privileged to be grafted into it but were not the initial recipients. They have been joined to a covenant with the sons of Jacob. The New Covenant that Jesus mentioned during the Last Supper is not primarily a gift to the Church but a promise – found in the Old Testament – made to the children of Israel.

The New Covenant takes its whole meaning when one sees it from the perspective of the Mosaic covenant. God promises to provide a new way to be in a righteous relationship with Him after His people have failed to keep the law. God doesn't abandon His people or give up on the righteousness of His law. He keeps both. He doesn't replace His people or change His desire for righteous living. God does a new thing: He provides more resources to empower His people to walk in the righteousness of the law before Him (Romans 8:4).

God pledges to establish a new relationship based on the foundation of the forgiveness of sins – the work of Jesus. Having taken care of their iniquity and broken the power of sin, He confirms that the house of Israel will know Him from within – the work of the Holy Spirit. He guarantees that He will write His law upon their heart, and He will be their God.

Prayer

Our Father,

We bless Your Holy Name. We praise You for making a New Covenant with the House of Israel. We worship you for Your gentleness in providing all the means for Your people to obey You. We thank You for allowing the believers of the nations to be part of this marvelous covenant.

We praise You for establishing forgiveness as the foundation of our relationship with You. We are not under condemnation. You have given us hope that our relationship with You doesn't end with our sins. We praise You for the forgiveness of sins through the sacrifice of Your Son. We thank You for the Holy Spirit who enables us to live a godly life before Your eyes.

Open the eyes of the Jewish people. Let them see that the New Covenant belongs to them. Let them discover that the coming of Jesus, the Lamb of God who takes away the sins, transforms everything in their relationship with You. Let them hear Jesus' words: "Come to me! My yoke is easy, and my burden is light."

In the Name of Jesus. Amen

DAY 14

THE GIFTS AND THE CALLING OF GOD ARE IRREVOCABLE

"And so, all Israel will be saved, as it is written: "The Deliverer will come out of Zion, And He will turn away ungodliness from Jacob; For this is My covenant with them, When I take away their sins." Concerning the gospel, they are enemies for your sake, but concerning the election they are beloved for the sake of the fathers. For the gifts and the calling of God are irrevocable."

Romans 11:26-29 NKJV

<u>All Israel will be saved!</u> What a massive statement! The salvation of the whole nation of Israel is part of <u>God's covenant</u> with them. God ensures that all will be saved, not only a remnant. This remarkable promise to Israel is part of God's covenant; not all nations will be entirely saved.

God has not given up on His firstborn people. He is forever faithful to His covenant with them. He knows that the outcome will be glorious. God has prepared a most emotional reconciliation between Israel and His Son Jesus and, following it an extraordinary salvation! They will see the One they pierced (Zachariah 12:10).

The apostle Paul states that they are – temporarily – enemies of the Gospel, but concerning the election, they are beloved. Their opposition does not cancel God's sovereign choice. Israel remains the beloved chosen people for the sake of their fathers. The gifts and calling of God for Israel are irrevocable because His covenants remain forever. The unfaithfulness and unbelief of Israel do not cancel her gifts and calling. This promise pertains initially and primarily to Israel and not firstly to a minister in crisis.

The certainty of Israel's salvation at the end of the story should not lure the Church into the snare of inaction. It is essential to reach out to the Jewish people and share the Gospel with them, even if it is not welcome initially. Praying for the supernatural revelation of Jesus, visions, and angelic visitations is essential. It is reported that, as in the Muslim world, many Jews are drawn to their Messiah through dreams and other supernatural activities.

Note: In this passage, Apostle Paul is referring to Isaiah 59:20-21 and Jeremiah 31:31-34

Prayer

Our Father,

We bless Your Holy Name. We praise You for guaranteeing the salvation of all Israel at the end of the story. We worship You for Your faithfulness to Your covenants. We celebrate You for preparing the reconciliation of Israel with Your Son Jesus. We love You for not giving up on Israel despite her unfaithfulness and unbelief. It gives us hope for our lives and the boldness to pray for the Jewish people.

We pray for the salvation of all Israel. Standing on Your promise, we agree with You and ask that You save all Israel. We pray that the current generation will see what Jesus has done for her, accept the forgiveness of her sins, and be saved. We pray for God to send laborers into this harvest field. We pray for You to strengthen and anoint the Messianic remnant in Israel who face much pressure for sharing the Good News with their Israeli compatriots.

We pray that the Body of Christ will understand the gifts and calling of God for Israel. We pray that the worldwide Church will acknowledge that they are irrevocable and draw the correct conclusions concerning her relationship with Israel.

In the Name of Jesus. Amen

WEEK 3

GOD'S LOVE FOR JERUSALEM

You will arise and have compassion on Zion

DAY 15

GOD HAS CHOSEN JERUSALEM FOR HIS HABITATION

"The LORD swore to David a sure oath from which he will not turn back: "One of the sons of your body I will set on your throne. If your sons keep my covenant and my testimonies which I shall teach them, their sons also forever shall sit upon your throne." For the LORD has chosen Zion; he has desired it for his habitation: "This is my resting place forever; here I will dwell, for I have desired it."

Psalm 132:11-14 RSV

God has chosen Zion; He has desired it for His habitation. God declares that Jerusalem is His resting place <u>forever</u>. He will dwell there, for He has desired it.

God has a unique relationship with Jerusalem. Zion receives more attention than any other city. God has desired to live in Jerusalem, so much so that He will have His resting place there forever.

The Scriptures teach that God's manifest presence is in distinctive places, at particular times, with specific people. God was present at the crossing of the Red Sea, at the time of the Exodus, with Moses and the children of Israel. During the following year, He was no longer there; He was leading His people in the wilderness.

Someone influenced by a Greek mindset has a hard time picturing God in time and space because, in this worldview, the deity is an ethereal concept. The Bible shows that God has a personality with various emotions, desires, ways, and relationships affecting His decisions and actions.

Popular wisdom says: "Show me your house, and I will tell you who you are!" God dwells not in a house but in a city. Jerusalem is full of His story. It was the place of Abraham's sacrifice and the city and throne of David. It was the temple's location where crowds of worshippers gathered during the feasts. Jesus died and God resurrected Him in Jerusalem. Zion was the city where the Holy

Spirit was first poured out. In the future, among other events, Jerusalem will witness the appearing of Jesus, the salvation of the Jewish people, and the crushing of the Antichrist's armies. Yes, God has a special love for Jerusalem and has chosen to live there forever.

Prayer

Our Father,

We bless Your Holy Name. We thank You for making Yourself known to us. We love to get to know who You are, what is precious to You, what You feel, and what You think. Thank you for revealing Your love for Jerusalem so that we can get in alignment with Your choice.

We pray for the peace of Jerusalem (Psalm 122:6). We pray for Your will to be done in this city as it is in Heaven. We pray for the worldwide Church to understand Your heart and purposes for Jerusalem.

In the Name of Jesus. Amen.

DAY 16

JERUSALEM WILL BE CALLED THE THRONE OF GOD

"At that time, Jerusalem shall be called The Throne of the LORD, and all the nations shall be gathered to it, to the name of the LORD, to Jerusalem. No more shall they follow the dictates of their evil hearts."

Jeremiah 3:17 NKJV

73

God has a glorious future for Jerusalem related to His presence in her. Jeremiah sees that she will be called the throne of the Lord, although he lamented the abundance of her sins in his time. God has the plan to transform Jerusalem entirely through His glory. She will be known as a place where God rules. His presence will change hearts; they will reject evil. Sin will have no more power.

The Shekinah glory of the Lord will not only be in the temple but over the whole city. God will establish His government over Jerusalem. Once rebuked for her rebellion by the prophets, this capital will be an example of righteousness. God will demonstrate His zeal and transforming power in Jerusalem. She will be a trophy of grace in His hand.

God will reign from Jerusalem, and all nations will gather to His throne, the Lord's name, and Jerusalem. Is there any more explicit evidence that Jerusalem has a special place in God's heart? All the people will see and acknowledge that God has a unique love for Jerusalem, and they will actually come to the city. The most hostile nations to Israel will not only gather to the Lord, but they will gather to Jerusalem. All the peoples will submit to the government of God and align with His sovereign choice of Jerusalem. Their hearts will be set free from evil.

Prayer

Our Father,

We bless Your Holy Name. We praise You for Your heart and plan for Jerusalem. She will be called the throne of the Lord. We thank You for this demonstration of Your jealousy and its transforming power. Jerusalem will be a trophy of Your persevering love.

We pray that You will enlighten the hearts of Your children all over the earth. Let them see the glorious future of Jerusalem, the city You love so much. Let them understand how Your zealous love can transform a sinful city into a place of Your glory.

We pray that You protect Your children from the spirit of the age and from siding with those who hate Jerusalem or with those who write her off because of her current rebellion against You.
We pray for the Jewish people to encounter Jesus, their Messiah, and be transformed into His image.

In the Name of Jesus. Amen.

DAY 17

JERUSALEM WILL BE A CROWN OF GLORY IN THE HAND OF THE LORD

"For Zion's sake I will not hold My peace, and for Jerusalem's sake I will not rest, Until her righteousness goes forth as brightness, And her salvation as a lamp that burns. The Gentiles shall see your righteousness, And all kings your glory. You shall be called by a new name, Which the mouth of the LORD will name. You shall also be a crown of glory In the hand of the LORD, And a royal diadem In the hand of your God. You shall no longer be termed Forsaken,

Nor shall your land any more be termed Desolate; But you shall be called Hephzibah, and your land Beulah; For the LORD delights in you, And your land shall be married. For as a young man marries a virgin, So shall your sons marry you; And as the bridegroom rejoices over the bride, So shall your God rejoice over you."

Isaiah 62:1-5 NKJV

God unveils His passionate affection for Zion. He desires to see her righteousness shining brightly. He commits to working unceasingly until her salvation glows like a burning lamp. God will be so pleased with Jerusalem that He wants all the kings to see her glory. His great joy about her will not remain private; it will go public. He wants to present her to the nations like king Ahasuerus took pride in showing the beauty of his queen to all his guests of honor.

God promises to call Jerusalem by a new name. She will no longer be named "Forsaken," but she will be called "My delight is in her." Her land will no more be labeled "Desolate" but "Married." Is not a love story – in all purity and holiness – the best way to describe this story between God and Jerusalem? The heart of a delighted husband radiates all through this scripture.

God bestows prophetic praises and life-giving compliments on Zion. He proclaims that she shall be a crown of glory and a royal diadem in His hand. God is exceptionally proud of Jerusalem. He declares her beauty and treats her like a queen. He rejoices over her as the bridegroom rejoices over his bride!

Prayer

Our Father,

We bless your Holy Name. We praise You for Your desire and commitment to see Jerusalem's righteousness shine brightly. We thank You for changing her name from "Forsaken" to becoming "My delight is in her." Your love gives her a new identity.

We pray for the righteousness of Jerusalem to go forth. We pray for her salvation.

We pray for the Jewish people who feel that You have forsaken them. Open their eyes to Your love. Let them know that You delight in them. Show them that You work tirelessly for their salvation.

In the Name of Jesus. Amen.

DAY 18

I HAVE SET WATCHMEN ON YOUR WALLS, O JERUSALEM

"I have set watchmen on your walls, O Jerusalem; They shall never hold their peace day or night. You who make mention of the LORD, do not keep silent, And give Him no rest till He establishes And till He makes Jerusalem a praise in the earth."

Isaiah 62:6-7 NKJV

God has set sentinels on the walls of Jerusalem. He has chosen to partner with intercessors to make Jerusalem a praise in the earth. God could do it all by Himself, but that is not who He is. He likes to have His children involved in His work. He enjoys sharing His plans and engaging His intercessors to make His dreams reality on earth.

God needs dedicated watchmen who will cry out to Him day and night. The intercessors for Jerusalem – as a group all over the earth – are on call 24/7. They need to be available day and night. Their task is so vital that they should never stop praying. Interceding for Jerusalem is one of the main reasons for building 24/7 houses of prayer.

God instructs His watchmen: "I want to hear your voices day and night. Don't give me rest until I make Jerusalem a praise in the earth. Do not be shy; do not be concerned about disturbing My tranquility. Do not hesitate to keep Me awake and come before Me repeatedly. You are doing My work." There is a unique complicity between God and His night and day intercessors for Jerusalem. He assures them that He does not rest as they do not take a break.

Prayer

Our Father,

We bless Your Holy Name. We praise You for Your plans for Jerusalem. We thank You for partnering with Your intercessors to fulfill Your will for Zion. Thank you for sharing with Your children what matters most to You. We so appreciate the honor.

We pray for 100 million intercessors for Jerusalem and Israel to be raised all over the earth. We pray that Your worldwide Church will take Jerusalem's destiny to heart and join You until she becomes a praise in the world.

We pray for houses of prayer interceding and worshipping 24/7 to emerge all over the planet. Let Your Church become a praying body partnering with Your heart and purposes.

We pray for the salvation of the Jewish people. We pray that You call and send messengers of Good News to them. We pray that You confirm their testimony with signs and wonders.

In the Name of Jesus. Amen

DAY 19

GOD WILL COMFORT THE LOVERS OF ZION IN JERUSALEM

""Rejoice with Jerusalem, And be glad with her, all you who love her; Rejoice for joy with her, all you who mourn for her; That you may feed and be satisfied With the consolation of her bosom, That you may drink deeply and be delighted With the abundance of her glory." For thus says the LORD: "Behold, I will extend peace to her like a river, And the glory of the Gentiles like a flowing stream. Then you shall feed; On her sides shall you be carried, And be dandled on her knees. As one whom his mother comforts, So I will comfort you; And you shall be comforted in Jerusalem.""

Isaiah 66:10-13 NKJV

85

There is great joy awaiting those who love Jerusalem. Those who mourn for her will rejoice with her. They will partake in the joy of her glory as they have shared the pain of her affliction. The soldiers, who suffered because of the invasion of their country, were the ones who rejoiced the most on Liberation Day. Similarly, those who wept with the beloved city in her time of distress will be glad when they witness the abundance of glory that God will bestow on her. With the consolation she will receive, they will be satisfied – find peace and quietness for their soul - like a sucking baby.

When we sincerely and profoundly love someone, we are greatly comforted to see them getting well after a season of illness. Likewise, those who love Jerusalem will be comforted to see her ample peace, continuous well-being, and lavish prosperity. They will be consoled from the pain they felt for the city as they watch the extravagant consolation God has prepared for her. God makes clear that His comfort comes as He transforms the circumstances of Jerusalem. It is not only an inner reality.

God will comfort those who love Jerusalem as a mother comforts her child. This is a rare scripture using the language of motherhood to describe the extraordinary tenderness of God. The consolation will occur in Jerusalem: "You shall be comforted in Jerusalem." There will be gladness and delight for those who see the abundance of her glory.

Prayer

Our Father,

We bless Your Holy Name. We praise You for the extraordinary tenderness You will display to comfort those who love Jerusalem. You will not let their hearts remain with undressed wounds caused by the distress of Jerusalem. You will provide consolation beyond measure for them and your beloved city. You will not let down those who share Your love for Jerusalem. They will rejoice beyond measure when they see her stunning glory and wellbeing.

We pray that Your worldwide Church will see Jerusalem's unique place in Your heart. We pray that You impart Your love for Jerusalem, Israel, and the Jewish people to the Body of Christ on the earth.

We pray that the Jewish people will encounter Jesus, their Messiah, who will heal their broken hearts.

In the Name of Jesus. Amen.

DAY 20

THE GLORY OF THE LORD
WILL RISE UPON
JERUSALEM

"Arise, shine; for your light has come, and the glory of the LORD has risen upon you. For behold, darkness shall cover the earth, and thick darkness the peoples; but the LORD will arise upon you, and his glory will be seen upon you. And nations shall come to your light, and kings to the brightness of your rising. Lift up your eyes round about, and see; they all gather together, they come to you; your sons

89

shall come from far, and your daughters shall be carried in the arms. Then you shall see and be radiant, your heart shall thrill and rejoice; because the abundance of the sea shall be turned to you, the wealth of the nations shall come to you."

Isaiah 60:1-5 RSV

God will make His glory rise upon Jerusalem. He will be her light and make her shine over the nations. The Lord will arise upon Jerusalem, and His glory will be visible upon her. There will be a sharp contrast between Jerusalem and the peoples of the earth because, at that time, they will live in darkness. The nations will witness Jerusalem reflecting the brightness of God. They will not see the glory of the Lord directly; they will see it indirectly as the light of the sun reflected on the moon at night. As for Jerusalem, she will see God and His glory.

Jerusalem will rise as a light on the earth, and kings will be drawn to her brightness. The sons and daughters of Israel will gather in Jerusalem. Those living far away will come back home. God will orchestrate a joyful reunion. Jerusalem will rejoice like a mother who gathers her children after a long absence. Her heart will swell and burst with joy. God will channel the wealth of the nations to Jerusalem – gold, incense, camels, sheep, and free labor because the people will come and serve her.

Prayer

Our Father,

We bless Your Holy Name. We praise You because You will make Your glory rise upon Jerusalem. You will cause her to be a light to the nations, and she will shine for all to see. We worship You because You have prepared a marvelous restoration for Jerusalem.

We pray that You open the understanding of the Church worldwide to Your plans for Jerusalem. Let Your purposes for her become significant and relevant to Your children.

We pray that what is essential to You becomes increasingly important for the Body of Christ.

In the Name of Jesus. Amen

DAY 21

JERUSALEM, THE CITY OF THE GREAT KING

"But I say to you, do not swear at all: neither by heaven, for it is God's throne; "nor by the earth, for it is His footstool; nor by Jerusalem, for it is the city of the great King. "Nor shall you swear by your head, because you cannot make one hair white or black. "But let your 'Yes' be 'Yes,' and your 'No,' 'No.' For whatever is more than these is from the evil one."

Matthew 5:34-37 NKJV

Jesus declares that <u>Jerusalem is the city of the great King</u>. The great King refers to God (Ps 47:2; Ps 48:2; Ps 95:3; Mal 1:14) and not to David. Jesus confirms that Jerusalem has a unique status in the sight of God. She is His city, like no other.

Jerusalem is the city of God. That is why the whole world talks daily about this small city in the Middle East. Megacities with more people, influence, wealth, power, resources, and innovation do not get the same attention. God has set her in the center of the nations (Ezekiel 5:5).

Jerusalem has aroused the passions of the human heart like no other city. She has been in the middle of violent wars for centuries. She has been destroyed and razed to the ground several times. The Scriptures teach that Jerusalem will be at the center of yet another battle at the end of this age. All the nations will surround her and attack her, and then Jesus will deliver her and save His ancient people, the children of Israel. Jesus will reign from Jerusalem. God declares: "I have set my king on Zion, my holy hill." (Ps 2:6). Jerusalem plays a central role in God's plan to exalt His Son.

Prayer

Our Father,

We bless Your Holy Name. We praise You for choosing Jerusalem as Your city. We worship You for loving Your city so well. We wait and pray for the coming of Your Son Jesus to Zion, Your holy hill.

We pray that the Body of Christ will understand the importance of Jerusalem in Your end-time plans and partner with Your will. Lead us to pray for Jerusalem and Israel.

We pray that You raise up intercessors, as watchmen on the wall for Jerusalem, who will intercede and cry out for her day and night until she becomes a praise in the earth (Isaiah 62.6-7).

In the Name of Jesus. Amen

ABOUT THE AUTHOR

Pierre Bezençon was born in Switzerland. He and his wife Laurence earned their Masters in Divinity and have served God full-time as pastors and Bible teachers for over thirty-five years. They have authored several books.

Since 2018, Pierre has been an intercessory missionary at the International House of Prayer in Kansas City. He has been part of the Israel Mandate leadership team.

His passion is to communicate the Father heart of God.

To invite Pierre to speak, email pierrebezencon@ihopkc.org

Father,

pray for children ministry;
from nursery to teens — to bring
forth anointed workers with a heart
for children. To pour into them
the truths and promises of your heart
God.

Fill every service with workers who
are comitted to serve you Father and
share the Love of Christ with them;
plants dreams and seeds in their
hearts to serve you all the days of
their life.

Made in the USA
Monee, IL
29 April 2023